READ WHAT O
"TR

"Tragic Treasures is much more than your typical motivational or self-help book. The author, who completely bares her soul, takes her readers on a journey through some of the lowest points in her life. However, **this is no sob story, as she reveals that through tragedy there can be triumph.** After reading this book, you will be inspired to reevaluate the negative things you have been through to find your own spiritual lessons."
~Raphael Baker, Editor-in-Chief of Rags 'N' Riches Magazine

"**.... Guaranteed to touch the lives of many while giving us the motivation** to re-evaluate our struggles.... **I was deeply moved with the ability to relate to her journey.** Her story has truly blessed and inspired me in many ways. **I would HIGHLY recommend this book....** ~ *Tiffanie Minnis, Author of the upcoming novel D.I.V.A.- Domestically Involved in Violent Affairs*

"The well written inspirational message in **Tragic Treasures will lift even the most despondent spirit....** I am a fan of her work."
~Elysa, Author of "Metaphorical"

"**....The "Word's" you've shared are pertinent and life changing....**" *~Elder Julius R. Speller Jr.*

"**Tragic Treasures indubitably has the "Triple E" effect: Emotional, Enlightening and Empowering. A must read....**"
~Tasha

"**.... It was a powerful.... Excellent read.... a must have in your collection!** *~Elder A. Tyler, Baltimore, MD*

READ WHAT OTHERS ARE SAYING ABOUT
"TRAGIC TREASURES"

What can you say about a woman who's overcome enough heartache to fill ten lifetimes? Rosena is nothing short of amazing. From the time she loses her step-father at age of 10 to her stalking her own son to save him from the streets, Rosena shows great strength of character in always overcoming whatever life throws at her. Using Bible references throughout the book, and prayer at the end of each chapter, Rosena shows us how to overcome our own troubles. There is a place to write down our own decisions to examine our own lives as Rosena has done so with her own. If the 'unexamined' life is not worth living, then this book can help anyone on the road to finding what matters and setting a course towards the light.

Stunning in its honesty, the author of Tragic Treasures finds salvation by first finding the bottom. **Rosena takes us on her very personal journey to the 'dark night of the soul' and emerges a warrior for the light.** Making us all see that maybe our own lives aren't so bad considering what this brave woman had to endure. **They say that the greater the light, the darker the shadow, which means that Rosena is now one of the brightest lights we have. Great story of a great woman.**

~Robin Landry, Author of "When I Dream"

Tragic Treasures:

Discovering Spoils of War in the Midst of Tragedy

Peace & Blessings
always,
Di

Tragic Treasures:

Discovering the Spoils of War in the Midst of Tragedy

Copyright © 2010 by Dianne Rosena Jones

Cover Design by Elena Covalciuc Vieriu

DISCLAIMER

This book is designed to provide information in regards to the subject matter covered. The purpose of the book is to educate and entertain. The author, editor, and publisher shall have neither liability nor responsibility to any person or entity with respect to any loss or damaged caused, or alleged to be caused, directly or indirectly by information contained in this book.

FOR MORE INFORMATION

For information about Royal Treasures Publishing, go to www.royaltreasurespublishing.com or send an email to: info@royaltreasurespublishing.com or write: Royal Treasures Publishing, P.O. Box 3136, Duluth, GA 30096

Table of Content

ᚼ

Dedications

Branden: May you find the treasure that God has hidden in your earthen vessel. I am grateful to my Creator for blessing me with you. Although we've had to fight the Adversary and sometimes we inadvertently fought each other, I hope you know just how much I love you. You thrived in a damaged womb, where your siblings could not survive. CHOSEN by God to come forth and LIVE. This book is dedicated to you, and so am I.

Dora: Your love transcended the womb. You loved me from the womb of another woman. You were never barren. You withstood the sickness, pain, suffering, and blame from Doctor's report, heart attacks, and strokes. Thank you for "fighting the Spirit of Death" and surviving for the first 17 years of my life. I miss you every day. I will love you forever.

Annette: For years, I could not see beyond the tragedies of our childhood long enough to have a real relationship with you. For too many years, I shut you out of my life. I thank God for reconciling us. I have always loved you. Forgive me for not being there. I am here now. You're Baby Sis.

Acknowledgments

To: Dee Stewart, Linda Dominique Grosvenor, Elena C. Vieriu, and Stephen Evans thanks for your excellence and your expertise.

Mac: I don't think I ever thanked you for fighting the Spirit of Suicide you saw overtaking me that day in 1981. I was so upset over the tactics you used. All I can say today is thank you. I will never forget "the gun" that saved my life.

Eva: God gave us a relationship only He could forge. Thank you for loving my son as your own. Thank you for always being supportive of everything I do. I love you. Truly, we are a family "blended" by God.

To My Sista's in the Spirit (Turshandah, Linda, Alicia, Janet, & Sherrie): I am sustained because of your prayers. We have prayed, praised, played, laughed, and cried together. Thank you for unconditional love. Thanks for telling me when I am wrong and picking me up when I fall. Thanks for being the family of my dreams.

Jethro Coe Jr.: In October 1988 when I returned from the psychiatric ward after suffering an emotional breakdown God used you to speak "life" to my dying spirit. The words you spoke into my life changed the course of my destiny. I am eternally grateful.

Sheila: Thank you for dressing me, crying with me, and sticking by me, when everyone else knew I had "lost my mind." You stuck with me until "I found it." We truly are sisters despite racial differences. We always will be.

Bishop Vincent L. Cornish: God used you to facilitate spiritual restoration in my life. Thank you for leading me back to my Heavenly Father. Thank you for 12 years of spiritual guidance, love, and support. I am eternally grateful for the difference you made in my life. Rest in Peace.

Maurice: You gave me the support I needed at a critical time in the process of birthing this book. For that I am eternally grateful.

Introduction

CB

Have you experienced a tragedy so difficult that you struggled trying to find any meaningful purpose whatsoever in your pain? Recalling those memories left you emotionally wounded all over again? Heartbroken and spiritually weakened by the mental attacks associated with the tragic event? So preoccupied with the loss you overlooked the possibility of hidden treasures? Pretending to be healed, but unable to release the pain and move on? Ignoring life lessons because you didn't understand the packaging they came in?

It's time to confront the ghost of your past. Expose and release damaging recollections by the power of the Spirit within you. Allow life altering events to shift your consciousness towards spiritual illumination. Prevent the loss of hopes and dreams. Find unconditional love and forgiveness amidst the debris.

Tragic Treasures

Develop a spiritual posture receptive to Divine guidance. Employ spiritual weapons of mass destruction. Cultivate the fruit of the Spirit which will cause you to transcend the tragedy and grow in grace. Accelerate the healing process by discovering spiritual treasures. Channel justifiable emotions into a righteous cause which brings about positive changes.

Walk out your life empowered by your victories not tormented by your defeats. Learn how to embrace and share life lessons which propel you towards fulfilling your purpose. Rise above the tragic consequences of life, achieve enlightenment, and effortlessly reach your destiny.

Begin your treasure hunt today and discover hidden treasures in the midst of every tragic moment.

Chapter One

Purpose in Pain

☙

In the midst of tragedy objectivity is hard to find. Like most of us I have endured many tragic moments. And I struggled for years, to find purpose from that pain. But instead of finding illumination from that struggle, I found a deeper struggle that caused internal conflicts which affected every area of my life. It hindered my emotional and spiritual growth for a number of years.

The tragedies left me emotionally wounded to the point where all I could focus on was the pain. I did my best to hide my wounds behind a façade of strength. The psychological attacks associated with the events weakened my spiritual core [mind, heart, and spirit]. A brief stay in a Psychiatric Ward provided the determination I needed to renew my core. Once mentally uncovered my quest for inner healing began.

Tragic Treasures

One day I read a story which elevated my level of thinking and switched the direction of my focus. It was the story about the battle of King Jehoshaphat[1] that helped me to see this.

*"And when Judah came toward the watch tower in the wilderness, they looked unto the multitude, and, behold, there were **dead bodies** fallen to the earth, and none escaped. And when Jehoshaphat and his people came to take away the **spoils** of them, **they found among them in abundance both riches with the dead bodies, and precious jewels**, which they stripped off for themselves, more than they could carry away: and **they were three days in gathering the spoil, it was so much.**"* [2]

After reading that story I wondered what hidden riches had been buried underneath my pain. At that moment, my own treasure hunt began. Basking in the Presence of God, our Creator empowered me with the courage to pursue and recover the Spoils of War left behind on the battlefield of life.

---

[1]. The Holy Bible: The King James Version [KJV]
[2] II Chronicles 20:1-37 KJV

11

Purpose in Pain

In my pursuit I discovered *hidden treasures* beneath the debris. Many of these treasures went unnoticed because they lie in midst of dead things. Dead things are negative memories and emotions associated with the tragic moment which prevent healing. In reading the Bible I realized that some of my life's lessons were obscured by corpses.

In my attempt to manage the grief process, I implemented a plan to distance myself from my tragedies. I tried to forget it all desperately. However, forgetting the pain couldn't open the doors for me to learn from the experience, to heal, and to forgive the past. Life battles whether won or loss should never be forgotten. We should remember the Wars we have fought. We should celebrate every victory and record every defeat. Evoking only dead things [negative memories of things lost] leave us stuck with the harmful memory of being conquered.

So I began a journey to transform my memories. I couldn't change the past, but I would revolutionize the outcome, by adjusting my thoughts. My journey required I go back in my psyche to the horrific scene of many tragic moments in my life that left me feeling defeated. I had to revisit that place, in order to release the pain tied to those memories. I had gone back to those moments many times before, but in the past my focus wasn't to find hidden treasures. Reminiscing left me wounded all over again.

THIS TIME with God's perfect plan in place, THE OUTCOME WOULD BE DIFFERENT.

I began my TREASURE HUNT almost sixteen years ago. It was far from easy. At times I wanted to give up. Sometimes I just quit. I've had to fight to "recover" every valuable treasure I left behind, and it's far from over. It's a part of our soul's journey that never ends. The story of King David in the Bible gave me incentive to continue despite life's setbacks. King David was an imperfect man who committed heinous crimes. Despite his flawed character when he lost everything to his enemies, God[3] encouraged him to do two

things: PURSUE & RECOVER ALL.

"So David and his men came to the city, and behold, it

*was **burned with fire; and their wives, and their sons, and***

***their daughters, were taken** captives. Then David and the*

people that were with him lifted up their voice and wept, until

*they had no more power to weep. And **David was greatly***

***distressed…because the soul of the people was grieved.** And*

David enquired of the Lord, saying, shall I pursue after this

*troop? Shall I overtake them? And he answered him, **Pursue:***

for thou shalt surely overtake them, and without fail recover

all. *"* [4]

No matter how devastating life has been **it's never too**

late to PURSUE & RECOVER ALL.

---

[3] I Samuel 30:3-4, 6, and 8
[4] I Samuel 30:3-4, 6, New King James Bible

Tragic Treasures
Divine Spirit,

I must admit that I've struggled trying to find true purpose in pain. Today I open my mind, my heart, and my spirit as I embark upon this journey of self discovery.

&

Take a moment and think of things that have caused you pain. Write those things on this page. Be honest with yourself. No one will see this except you. Why it causes you pain doesn't matter, right now. Who was to blame is not relevant. What you should have done is not important. Just be honest with yourself. Make a list of those things that still bring you pain.

_____

_____

_____

_____

_____

_____

Chapter Two
Tragic Moments

ଓଷ

"But we have this treasure in earthen vessels that the Excellency of the power may be of God and not of us. We are troubled on every side, yet not distressed. We are perplexed, but not in despair; persecuted, but not forsaken; cast down, but not destroyed." II Corinthians 4:7-9

No one has escaped life's tragic moments. How we respond to those tragedies sets us apart. Some of us have survived, while others have become overwhelmed to the point of ending their lives. The good news is that those who survived may have been cast down but not destroyed. I will not attempt to define what one considers a tragedy. Tragic moments are personal to each of us. Tragic moments are not easily defined or effortlessly forgotten. They range from the loss of a loved one to the betrayal of a friend; from the loss of a job to a debt increase; from infidelity and divorce to mental illness or physical abuse. I have suffered through rejection, serious illness, abandonment, death, molestation, miscarriage, depression, divorce, betrayal, infidelity, emotional and mental abuse, debt, repossession, and eviction. I even survived being stalked and having my life threatened. Most of these tragic moments happened more than twenty years ago, and I survived.

To tell the truth, I had taken this chapter out of the book many times. I feared it was too graphic, too tragic, and too depressing to share. I know that for some the truth is not always easy to receive. However, this is MY TRUTH and it must remain, to help you. I cannot change my history, it has already been written by my living. This chapter will give you some insight into some of the tragic moments I've faced in life. Some battles I won and some I lost. Some treasures I have recovered and others I am still in search of. I'm still learning to walk in the power of my victories. Take comfort in the revelation that even in defeat there are hidden treasures to be discovered. I've chosen to remove my mask and speak openly about my failures, disappointments, and tragedies. I hope you will discover, pursue, and recover your hidden treasures.

Tragic Moments

Despite the rubbish of every perceived failure, disappointment, and tragedy in your life never forget the Spoils of War.

Often when I share the details of my existence, I mention the loss of seven loved ones in eight years. Six of those deaths occurred within a two and a half year time period. To summarize those years, when I was ten-years-old my adopted father died from a massive heart attack during a hernia operation. At fifteen my natural mother [who literally gave me away at birth] died suddenly in my sister's arms at our front door. Two weeks after the death of my natural mother, my five-month old niece had open heart surgery and died of heart failure. I will never forget riding in the Limousine with her little casket on the front seat, because it was too small for a hearse.

By the end of the year, I was sixteen and pregnant. I was startled to find out one unmemorable sexual encounter in the back seat of a car would result in pregnancy. Frankly I couldn't tell if we really had intercourse. The only evidence I saw was my wet skirt. I was inexperienced, naïve, and obviously ill informed. When I found out I was pregnant, I was horrified and for good reason. I was the adopted daughter of a devout Holiness-Pentecostal, Hell-Fire-and-Brimstone Evangelist. I was convinced if she ever found out I was pregnant she would throw me out of the house. She had thrown my sister out of the house for less. Because I had always felt rejected and abandoned by my natural mother, I couldn't bear the thought of losing my adopted mother's love as well. I wasn't concerned about the baby, and I was too immature to understand that my behavior was a symptom of grief that I had yet to address. I didn't want to lose my mom's love; I couldn't. So when I started to miscarry I thought, my momma would never have to know her baby girl had disappointed her.

What I didn't plan on was the possibility of my bleeding to death. Four weeks later the bleeding hadn't stop. In fact, it had become uncontrollable and hard to hide. I couldn't go to school. I made up excuses to stay home. It didn't take long for my sister to realize I was pregnant. I begged her to keep my secret. One day I was in so much pain until my mom called the paramedics, but I refused to allow them to examine me. I lied when they asked me if I was pregnant, so they left. And thus, I continued to bleed. The cramping tortured me. I became so weak I could barely get out of the bed. I will never forget the day I lost my baby. The doctor said I lost so much blood I needed a blood transfusion. I should have been thankful, but I was more afraid for my life than ever.

Momma now knew my secret. I anticipated the worse when she came to my room. Instead she held my hand and kissed my forehead without speaking a word. She NEVER spoke a negative word to me concerning the entire ordeal up until the day she died, despite her reputation for telling it like it is. That day I saw unconditional love in its purest form.

Fifteen months later mom slipped into a diabetic coma and died from septic shock. I was orphaned at seventeen. I barely made it through my senior year of high school. I married the first man who said he loved me. Although I'd known my husband since I was twelve, I married him out of desperation. I feared being alone.

Tragic Treasures

In August 1981 one month after my mom passed, my nephew was born premature with the top of his skull still open. My sister never got to hold him in her arms. One of the nurses took a picture of him from the neck down and gave it to her. He lived only seven hours. While still trying to come to terms with the death of my mother and my nephew, I received more catastrophic news. That news sent me spiraling into an overwhelming abyss of despair. I was overwhelmed by a spirit of depression.

By then, I was five months pregnant with my second child. When we went to my regular prenatal appointment the doctor couldn't find the baby's heartbeat. An ultra-sound revealed that our baby had died in my womb. It was nothing like the first time. There was no warning. No cramps. No pain. No blood. I was admitted into the hospital where they would proceed to take our dead baby from my womb.

Afterwards, my uterus was empty but in the womb of my spirit I carried "dead things" for much longer than five months. I left the hospital, went home, and stayed in the bed for the next month.

My days were filled with pain pills and my nights with sedatives. All I could do was weep uncontrollably day after day to the point that my soul was exhausted from grief. I remember the day that the thoughts of ending my life conquered my mind and poured out into my reality. With little effort I could end the torment by taking all the prescription medication. I longed to drift from sleep into eternity because the sorrow besieged my every waking moment.

I was convinced that my husband didn't see the true depths of my despair. We barely spoke during that dark time. He refused to discuss the baby at all. To me he acted as if our baby never existed. I felt he had become quite efficient at ignoring my tears and overlooking my anguish. I was wrong. But at the time I couldn't see past my own pain.

So the day came, and he left for work as usual with our only car. I was accustomed to him working 12 to 16 hour days without coming home for lunch. After he left, I took every pill

Tragic Treasures

I could find and got back in the bed. My actions weren't a cry for help or a scheme devised for attention. I couldn't take it anymore. My heart was broken and my spirit was crushed, BUT GOD intervened that day.

That day my husband came home for lunch. By all appearances I was merely sleeping. There was no empty pill bottles, no glass or suicide note. But he knew instinctively that I was dying. In the only way he knew how, he began to scream at me to wake up. He pulled me from the bed and dragged me into the kitchen. He forced milk down my throat. He continued forcing me to drink more and more milk until I began to vomit. I threw up continuously until I experienced dry heaves.

After I finished vomiting, my husband went and got his handgun. He brought the loaded gun and sat it down in front of me. With anger in his voice, he said, "If you are going to kill yourself, stop fucking around, and do it." I was shocked and appalled. He wouldn't allow me to go back to sleep for hours. His insensitivity angered me. I survived, but I was different. I

23

Tragic Moments
hid all of my emotions deep inside. In the years that followed I

would emotionally implode.

Divine Spirit,

There are some tragic moments in my life that no one knows about. I have carried some of them covered in mystery under the fear of discovery. Some of these moments still cause me great pain and others cause me a considerable amount of shame. Help me, as I prepare to embark on a journey that will change my life forever. I need freedom from the emotional turmoil attached to these traumatic memories.

&

You've listed some things that cause you pain. Go back and look at your list. Did you leave some things off the list? Things you've never mentioned and surely never written down. Secrets you've never shared with anyone? List the tragic events that changed you forever. You may need to go back in the recesses of your mind and start with your childhood. Maybe you really don't believe that it affected you, but now, it's time to admit to yourself that it did. Write it down.

_____

_____

_____

_____

Chapter Three

We Wear the Mask

I fell in love with *"We Wear the Mask"* when I attended college Morgan State University. It spoke to the depths of my soul and has remained there. "We wear the mask that grins and lies. With torn and bleeding hearts we smile." It captured my attention because although it was written for a different era, a different people, it defined my existence. I had not endured slavery or experienced fear and torture during the time of Jim Crow, but I knew what slavery felt like, emotionally. Paul Lawrence Dunbar penned how I felt, each time I smiled while silent cries rose from my torn and bleeding heart.

He also shared how most former slaves survived emotionally during this time. They wore "the mask." It hid their outrage and covered their anger. It enabled them to survive the carnage of their reality. For those who survived 400+ years of Slavery "the mask" was vital to their existence.

Although, the Slavery that our ancestors experienced is over, many of us remain psychologically imprisoned in countless ways. What was meant to protect us has now enslaved us. Our survival mechanisms have gone awry leaving us trapped behind a protective covering indefinitely. For me I thought that my mask had enabled me to live with my tragic past, but in all actuality, "I was trapped." I became trapped behind a facade that I embraced during a season of turmoil, because I could not find a way to detach myself from the experience. My defense mechanism was flawed. The tragic moment was over but I could not find my way out from behind my camouflage. I had no tools for emotional success.

I know exactly when I slipped behind my first mask. I came to realize that my brokenness over the death of my adopted mother and the loss of my second baby was too much for my husband to handle. I unrealistically expected my husband to be able to carry the weight of my sorrow, but he could not. He responded in the only way that he knew how in order to ensure his own emotional survival. He ignored my agony. He could not embrace the gravity of my pain. I understand his reaction now. I did not understand it then. It seemed as if my weakness embarrassed him and my tears angered him. I taught myself how to present an outward appearance which would not reveal my inner agony.

We had what appeared to be a good life together on the surface. We lived in Europe attended the Opera, and traveled to Paris, London, and Amsterdam. By the six[th] year of marriage we were living in Hawaii (Paradise) but secretly I was dying inside but I continued to wear the mask. My first long-term relationship taught me there was a pain so deep others could not carry the weight of "knowing."

After a while I began to believe that no one would understand my grief. I covered my pain more and my wounds grew deeper. It was like covering a stab wound with a band-aid. The wound may not have been be visible to others, but I was still bleeding to death inside.

Such tremendous loss caused me to question God's love. I started to look at my pain as some type of spiritual punishment. Once I believed the lie that God didn't love me, those thoughts crippled me psychologically. I became so disillusioned, until I actually feared that God would take everyone that I loved from me. I stopped going to church for fourteen years because at the time my association with God was strictly connected to church attendance. I felt unloved and grew angry at God.

On top of everything else, I developed abandonment issues. My abandonment issues led to a fear of rejection. I expected those I loved to leave me or worse die. In an attempt to cover the wounds further complicated by my feelings of rejection, I pretended not to be wounded at all. Then I carried the disguise to the next level by "acting" as if I were incapable of being hurt at all. That was the biggest lie of all. Sometimes it worked, but most of the time it just caused me to send mixed signals to the people in my life. In one moment, I would be gentle, caring, tearful, then in the next I would be cold and distant. Pretending to be unbreakable is very difficult when

you are already broken inside.

Divine Spirit,

Set me free from this self-imposed prison. I am so tired of hiding my pain. Every day, I wear a mask in a feeble attempt to protect my broken heart and camouflage my wounded spirit. I go through the motions, pretending to have joy when inside I am burdened by sorrow.

I have impersonated "wholeness" for so long until I do not know where the fantasy ends and the reality begins. I want to be "whole" for real. How do I take off the disguise I've worn for so long? Help me, to strip away all pretence to the point of becoming vulnerable in front of you. I have been frightened by the thought of becoming vulnerable in front of others. I know that my ability to come before you "naked" is the key that will unlock the door, and lead to my deliverance.

I know that my capacity to reveal weakness to you makes available your strength to me in return. The curtain has fallen on my final performance and I want to start removing each layer of this elaborate costume today. I need your strength to take off this mask for good. Allow me to eliminate my first layer with this heartfelt prayer and honest confession. My fear of disapproval and rejection from others led me to conceal my inner turmoil. Allow true freedom to begin today.

&

Take a moment and list the disguises that you hide behind. How do you present yourself to others? Are you always perceived as the strong one, tough, independent, or self-sufficient? Do you take pride in the fact that you don't need anyone? Do you consider crying a sign of weakness? Does being vulnerable in front of others frighten you? Are you the caregiver, the rescuer, superwoman, the knight in shining armor, or the shoulder everyone can cry on?

_____

_____

_____

_____

_____

Chapter Four
Tragic Consequences

☙

In the beginning I carried my emotional insecurities very well. However, by the age of twenty-seven, I spiraled out of control. Abandoning the development of my spiritual core left me vulnerable to making bad decisions with tragic consequences. My weakened spirit was no longer receptive to Divine guidance from the Spirit of God. I developed what doctors called "suicidal tendencies." By early 1988, I was a divorced, single parent. That year a huge tear appeared in my perfect costume, and I was left "psychologically" uncovered.

My destructive behavior and suicidal tendencies were at an all time high. I became disillusioned. I became entangled in a romantic relationship with a married man. Our first sexual encounter resulted in a fourth pregnancy for me. I had finally given birth to a baby boy during my marriage. My son was around 3 years old at this time. I made the decision to have an abortion. I could not bring myself to tell this man that I had become pregnant and I definitely couldn't tell him about my decision to terminate the pregnancy.

I was lost. I should have known that I was not emotionally stable enough to endure the aftermath of such an experience, but I did it anyway. I left the clinic hysterical. I sobbed uncontrollably the entire ride home. Emotional turmoil engulfed me. That turmoil must have been mistaken for physical pain, because the girl that was with me took me straight to the Emergency Room.

The physical pain had ended, but the mental anguish was destroying me. Once inside the Emergency Room I wouldn't allow the doctor to examine me. I could not bring myself to allow anyone to touch me. Without being able to do anything else the doctor sedated me, and sent me home with instruction to remain in bed for a couple of days. I gladly stayed in bed because I could not stop the grief and sorrow. It poured from my spirit as if an emotional dam had burst inside me. All I could do was sob and sleep.

Tragic Treasures

The loss was enormous and the guilt and shame was almost unbearable. A few days afterward I got out of the bed and tried to put the mask back on. I tried to go back to pretending that everything was okay. I couldn't. That mask never fit the same way again. The previous mask hid grief and sorrow; this mask included guilt and shame. It would be months before I would mention that baby to anyone and years before I could admit that I had taken that baby's life.

By October I had lived the type of destructive lifestyle without boundaries void of Divine guidance due to a broken spirit connection that allowed others the freedom to mistreat me. I was so good at putting up a front until I believed no one thought anything could make me crumble, not even the betrayal that was about to come. The adulterous affair had spiraled out of control and began to resemble something close to the movie "9 ½ weeks." Captivated by this man, our sexual exploits included drinking, drugs, strip clubs, and eventually threesomes. For his birthday, we had a threesome with my best friend. However, after that night, they continued to see each other sexually without my knowledge. When she told me of their affair, I lost my mask and my mind. Let's say I was temporarily insane. It's comical now, but it was traumatic then. The only way to describe my behavior at that moment is to compare it to the character that Glenn Close portrayed in the movie "Fatal Attraction."

There was a scene where she was sitting with a knife in her hand while pulling the light switch on the lamp. She kept clicking the light on and off, on and off. I don't think any actress has looked as crazy as she did at that very moment, well, except me. I felt like Joan Crawford from Mommy Dearest during her clothes hanger scene and Glenn Close from Fatal Attraction, all rolled up into one crazy person.

I began to break things and scream. I got a huge Butcher's knife from my kitchen drawer and just carried it around. It reminded me of the knife that Jason carried in the first "Friday the 13th" movie. I waited for the unsuspecting "Double Cheater" to enter the door. I loved that "Double Cheater" but now I was going to have to cut him. I would cut him deep. My mind was inundated with fear, rejection, pain, anger, and distress. In the midst of this emotional breakdown negative thoughts flooded my weakened mind until my rage turned inward.

Something within my heart broke and my spirit gave up. Suddenly I was dazed, but I knew that I would never hurt anyone. After putting the Butcher's knife down, I walked over all the broken trinkets, glass on the floor, and went in search of relief. I searched frantically, but couldn't find an adequate source. Liquor wouldn't do it and no illegal drugs were available. I didn't want to die, but I needed the torment in my mind to stop. I needed a distraction that would divert my attention from the hole in my soul from which anguish flowed. I found it. I found something that I thought would take my mind off of the mental agony by causing physical pain: a small razor blade.

I returned to the couch with a new focus alleviating one type of pain by causing another type of pain. I struggled to make my way back to the couch. I felt as if I would pass out. I sat on the couch crying. I sliced my forearms repeatedly. I felt

the pain. I saw the blood, but I couldn't stop. All of the tragic

moments of my life led me to that place at that time. I couldn't

envision myself picking up that broken, shattered, mask and

putting it back on ever again. I sliced and cried sliced and cried.

As darkness surrounded me, chaos consumed my mind, than

out of nowhere a still small voice spoke to my spirit.

"Call 911," the voice said.

I picked up the phone and called 911. I was in the

Army and living in Military Housing. The Military Police

showed up at my door before the "Double Cheater" could

return. Thank God, because I was about to "catch a case" over

somebody else's husband. Now, that was crazy.

On that day, my mask fell off and all the pretence from

years past caught up with me. I couldn't pretend anymore. My

married lover rushed to the hospital to find me on the

Psychiatric Ward under suicide watch. I begged him to explain

why he had hurt me to the core of my being. He shattered my

broken heart. He couldn't answer me. All he could do was cry. That day, we cried together.

I was released after three days in the Psychiatric Ward. Humiliated by the realization others had discovered that "superwoman" was a fake. I felt like the Wizard from the movie "The Wizard of Oz" when it was discovered he was merely an old man behind a curtain. Just like the Wizard, I was an imposter posing as someone great and mighty. I felt vulnerable returning to work. I reported for Physical Training (PT) early that morning in shorts and a short-sleeve T-shirt with huge white bandages covering the multiple lacerations to each forearm. I stood in formation feeling exposed. There was nowhere to hide.

I haven't attempted to cover up the scars on my forearms in years. They are barely noticeable now. Just like my internal wounds slowly over the past 20 years they healed and faded away. The memories associated with my scars also changed. I am no longer reminded of the agony and defeat felt at that moment in my life. Now I see the victory of the Light that shined in a dark place when the Spirit of God came beyond

the veil of tragedy and rescued me. Divine light ripped through

the depths of despair into the pinnacle of my pain and changed

me. I will never forget that moment when I heard the Spirit of

God speak to my broken, shattered heart with these words:

"Baby Girl, sometimes you outran my covering, but you never outran my love."

Tragic Treasures
Divine Spirit,

I've suffered through the tragic consequences of bad decisions in my life due to my broken spiritual connection to Divine guidance for the last time.

&

Take your time and think of some of the decisions that you made which had tragic consequences. Now write down how you could have handled that situation differently which may have lead to a more positive outcome.

_____

_____

_____

_____

_____

Chapter Five

Releasing the Skeletons

CB

Many of the tragic moments in my life played out in my mind like battles that were won or lost. On that mental Battlefield laid the remains from each War I had fought. I left the Battlefield emotionally wounded and spiritually defeated. I shut the door on the "dead things" left behind as if I had just thrown some old shoes into the closet. I accumulated more and more psychological corpses in my mental closet. Those dead things stayed for so long until they became skeletons.

We've all heard the expression of "having skeletons in your closet." We understand what someone is implying when they say, "I have skeletons in my closet." They mean that they encountered issues [events or behaviors] which left a memory not easily forgotten. The impact of the negative encounter was placed in a secretive mental compartment away from the scrutiny of others. To place the memory in a closet suggests the issue has been hidden, but not necessarily resolved. Guarded locations keep others out and sometimes are not easily accessible even to its owner. Now days, closets have become spacious rooms which rival bedrooms and other large living areas. For most of us, a closet is a relatively small space with limited access, one entryway, and no windows. Often the only access to someone's closet is through the bedroom, which is a private area inaccessible without permission.

I was afraid to take inventory of the skeletons I hid. I hadn't resolved a majority of the memories attached to those remains. I never spoke of being molested. I repressed it. I was too ashamed to discuss the abortion. There were skeletons that I did not recognize like my fear of dying young, and those I could not forget like being stalked.

The Spirit challenged me to invade my revered storeroom, where my skeletons had peacefully resided for years. I was accustom to opening the door just enough to toss whatever I was dealing with in, without looking then slamming

41

the door shut. I stood there, in the recesses of my mind by the power of the Spirit. The place that held all my deep dark secrets had become a crude Memorial. It was far from the Graveyard that I envisioned. Nothing was really buried. I saw psychological corpses lying scattered above ground. Memories that kept me bound to tragedy. I had to recognize, expose, and release them to be free. I was ready to confront the ghosts of my past.

In the spirit realm, I began tossing those skeletons around, which left my wretched memories in a disheveled stack of broken bones. I took those lifeless things accumulated and transferred them from my psychological warehouse to their final resting place. I needed peace from the pain of my past. My spirit was grieved to overwhelming levels. Sorrow slipped over into my subconscious. I would cry while asleep. My husband would wake me up, but I'd have no conscious memory of what caused my tears. My grief poured from the depths of my soul into the reality of my nights. Releasing those memories played a critical role in being able to work through the grief process. There would be no recovery without release.

I welcomed the final eulogy. I'd spent years fixated on the loss, without any acknowledgement or recognition of that which remained. It was time for my last tribute to past suffering. No more monuments would be erected or dedicated to lingering pain. I had to evict the skeletons of pain, loss, grief, sorrow, death, rejection, fear, abandonment, molestation, bad decisions, failed relationships, promiscuity, abortion, depression, suicide attempt, serious illness, and medical mistakes from the depository of my psyche. I exposed every lifeless damaging recollection to the power of the Spirit within me. In doing so, I became conscious of the fact that those memories (no matter how painful) no longer held me hostage. I was free from the captivity of disaster.

Each day I threw the door of my closet open and prayed the Spirit would empower me to expel a few more dusty bones. It was not easy. I realized that it was just a small part of the ongoing journey towards discovering the Spoils of War.

Releasing the Skeletons

Beyond those relics of pain revealed hidden treasures. I visited my mental closet everyday to ensure that no bones had gone undetected. I couldn't prevent loss, pain, or disappointment; but I could prevent dead things from cluttering my mind and lingering in my spirit.

There were skeletons that I had blocked access to because the memories associated with them were just too painful to recall. I had to seek the guidance of a Mental Health professional. There was no shame or sin in seeking the help of Mental Health professionals. I did not believe that attending counseling suggested any lack of faith. Seeking counseling when necessary implied that I comprehended the fact that sometimes a holistic approach is required in order to facilitate complete healing. Sometimes we pray, read the Word, and overcome all barriers; other times, we need to pray, fast, and attend counseling sessions [3 times per week].

Releasing skeletons required more than just going into my psyche and pulling out bad memories. Releasing the remains of past traumatic experiences involved

44

Tragic Treasures

acknowledgement [perhaps confrontation if necessary], repentance, and forgiveness. My spiritual core: mind, heart, and spirit had to be strengthened in order to embrace repentance and forgiveness. Until I was ready to embrace both, I wasn't ready to release the painful memories of the past. My inability to forgive kept me bound to dead things. I had to become "willing" to forgive others, forgive myself, and accept the forgiveness of others, including God. I had to acknowledge the role that I played and sincerely repent for the pain and suffering that I contributed to my existence and the existence of others. I acknowledged the guilt and shame associated with some of the bad decisions I made throughout my life, and then I released those feelings and memories.

Often we use the expression that the issue is "dead and buried." That statement is our feeble attempt at implying that the subject is over. That's also our way of ending any questions related to the incident. The reality is, in most cases, it's not dead and buried; merely hidden and unresolved. Denial is one reason why many of us have such large mental storerooms. We

45

Releasing the Skeletons

embraced the spirit of denial in order to protect the psyche. By the power of the Spirit of God within me, I worked my way through emotions like: denial, disbelief, shock, loss, pain, regret, fear, hatred, and un-forgiveness; to embrace acknowledgement, acceptance, forgiveness, repentance, and release. I realized that just like the Battles and struggles that we encounter during our lives will never end. Neither will the process of releasing skeletons. As long as there are Battles, there will always be victories and defeats. There will always be "dead things" that could potentially become skeletons. When we have learned the process of release, only then, can we prevent our mental closets from being cluttered with psychological debris from the Battle.

Tragic Treasures
Divine Spirit,

You know how many skeletons I have hidden in the secret closet of my mind. My mind truly is a Battlefield. The debris and clutter of my mental closet causes me to fear psychological injury if I open the door. I fear that I am not strong enough to walk among the dead things. Help me to confront and release these skeletons. By the power of the Spirit, I come against every emotion that hinders spiritual release such as denial, disbelief, shock, un-forgiveness, and fear. I embrace my divine ability to acknowledge and confront when necessary, accept, repent, forgive, and release dead things/skeletons.

Help me to walk in a spirit of repentance and forgiveness, which precedes true healing. I repent of the harm that I have caused others and myself. I accept the love and forgiveness of others. I forgive myself. I receive your forgiveness, your love, and your acceptance, Father. I am accepted in the Beloved. Thank you for the strength to walk tall among the corpses of my tragic past. Thanks for the freedom, which comes with a proper burial and goodbye. I say goodbye to guilt and shame. I say goodbye to heartache and pain. I say goodbye to the tragic relics of my past. Remove every dead thing from my psyche. Strengthen my spiritual core. Show me how to bury the past for the last time.

&

Take time and think about the skeletons that need to be released. Write a list of those things you need to release. Repent for your involvement [if any]. Receive forgiveness and accept forgiveness from God. Now, forgive everyone involved and release them from all responsibility for the pain you've suffered.

_____

_____

_____

_____

_____

_____

_____

Chapter Six

Secret Deliverance

 os

Sixteen years ago, I returned to my religious roots and started attending church services on a regular basis in an added attempt to strengthen my spiritual core. I had to admit sometimes living with the pain was easier than really dealing with the pain. The only thing more uncomfortable was being transparent in front of others. I was frightened by the idea of telling people [especially church folk] where God had really brought me from. Nevertheless, God mandated me to share my secret deliverance. Until then no one knew what I had been delivered from and I was content carrying my secrets. But the Spirit wasn't satisfied with my decision to hide the truth.

Once back in church I praised God and worshipped Him through dance all over the church, while desperately trying to keep my scars from showing. I wanted to release it all, but I was still afraid to tell it all.

Over time it started to appear that I had exchanged one mask for another. The Spirit of God arrested me for it. He never allowed me to walk in that level of hypocrisy. He required transparency from me.

However, my frankness challenged my church family, especially other spiritual leaders. I believed they felt they needed to withhold information about themselves to ensure a certain level of reverence and respect. How ridiculous. Unfortunately, those I respected were the ones who were not afraid to show their scars. I needed to see how other spiritual leaders had walked out their old lives toward a new level of victory. At first it was a challenge to reveal my secrets, even while writing this book. I was quite happy basking in the bliss of my secret deliverance.

God healed me from unimaginable tragedies. I knew that God was capable of healing us so completely until others would no longer see any signs of emotional disfigurement.

However, many of us have gone on to put up a "front" in an attempt to pretend that our wounds never existed at all. Yes, there is a Balm of Gilead[5] that healed the sinned-sick-soul and covered every wound, but most serious wounds still leave scars. The scars remind us of the battles we've won and lost. It is important to remember which battles were won and which were lost, **BECAUSE IT IS NEVER TOO LATE TO GAIN THE VICTORY OVER A PAST DEFEAT!**

We can live triumphantly despite all of life's tragic moments. We languish in defeat when we camouflage our emotions. Moreover, we prevent our spiritual wounds from completely healing. Victory is diminished when we hide our scars [real testimony] from others due to fear of rejection from man.

I came to the realization I may have been healed from the tragic moments of my past, but I was not walking in total deliverance if I still felt the need to keep a secret.

---

[5] Balm in Gilead is a reference in Genesis Chapter 37 and Jeremiah 46:7

Secret Deliverance

One day the Spirit asked me, "How would God be glorified in my secrecy?"

I could not answer that question. I knew I was the only one being glorified by my secrecy. Church folk always say, "To God be the Glory." Well, I had to evaluate whether I could keep my deliverance private and at the same time allow God to have His Glory.

The Holy Spirit revealed God receives no Glory whatsoever in my secrecy, no matter how loud I praised Him or how hard I danced at church. Healing had taken place, but my deliverance wasn't complete until I could walk in total freedom. I had to surrender my pride and my fear.

The secrecy was restricting the Spirit's ability to complete the process. I had been healed from the pain, but not delivered from the tragedy. I no longer felt the pain of the wound, but I had not surrendered the memories of the event.

Guarded memories prevented freedom to expose them. Surrendered memories, on the other hand, allowed deliverance. My spiritual independence flowed from the power of the Spirit to others thereby setting me free to share my real testimony with others who may have been defeated by the weight of their tragic secrets. I finally understood I would never reach my destiny until I was able to share the truth about my scars without restrictions and without fear. I had to walk in a level of transparency that could only be achieved with immeasurable healing. I would not truly emerge as the person God created me to be, if I remained, constrained by my secret deliverance.

Queen Esther's story is a wonderful example of secret deliverance. Esther[6] went from an orphaned Jewish girl to Queen over 127 provinces from India to Ethiopia without anyone knowing who she really was and where she came from. When Haman manipulated the King into approving a decree which gave him the authority to slaughter the Jewish people, Mordecai, Esther's uncle came to her and requested she reveal her identity to her husband, King Ahasuerus and plea for the life of her people.

---

[6] The Book of Esther Chapter 4

Secret Deliverance

The Queen hesitates at first and responds she would be risking her life if she attempted to go before the King uninvited. Mordecai tells his niece just perhaps, she had been positioned by God, in the Palace to do just that. God knew one day she would reveal where He had brought her from "for real" and it would be for the saving of her people. Queen Esther received the revelation and said she would go and see the King unannounced and if she perished then so be it. She went to the King, revealed her secret, and saved her people. Who knows? Revealing your secret deliverance to the right person in due season could save a life, including yours.

Tragic Treasures
Divine Spirit,

I've lived through some things others can barely comprehend. It's difficult to reveal all I've been delivered from. Once the wounds healed I covered the scars in my new robe of righteousness. It's difficult to get people to see beyond where you came from. I've been afraid to show my scars. It's much easier to keep it a secret and just celebrate my new life. Give me the strength to be transparent and the wisdom to know when.

&

Think about the tragedies in your life that you've overcome, but kept secret. List them.

_____

_____

_____

_____

_____

_____

Chapter Seven

Birthed Out

CB

A number of you may be familiar with the concept of being "birthed out." For those who are not familiar with the term to be "birthed out" implies that everyone goes through a period of spiritual gestation. This spiritual development could take a few months, a number of years, or a lifetime. This spiritual stage peaks with a release not unlike that of childbirth. This spiritual progression includes many attributes similar to pregnancy like growth, isolation, and labor pains. Being "birthed out" is but one juncture on the continuum of spiritual illumination. It is a spiritual evolution that I believe every human being experiences, even if they refuse to embrace traditional religion or ever attend a church service.

I want to discuss what I believe to be a universal process that I will refer to as being "birthed out." As with natural childbirth, complications do arise in the Spirit Realm. When difficulties surface during the gestation period, they could result in the spiritual equivalent of false labor, miscarriage, premature birth, developmental delays, physical limitations, and mental challenges. When spiritual obstacles are not attended to with divine precision and sensitivity, spiritual babies are born deformed or crippled. For those who ignore the warning signs when problems surface spiritual pregnancies could end in stillbirths.

Spiritual passage is vital towards Man's holistic journey. Some people embrace the ideology that the close spiritual connection between us and our Creator was damaged in the Garden of Eden due to The Fall. With that as the backdrop, some believe that the sum of Man's existence is to find his way back to the relationship that he possessed with his Creator in the Garden of Eden.

In other words, our main objective is to return to our pre-fallen state of existence. If you want to know what our pre-fallen state was read the first 3 chapter of the Book of Genesis.

Many believe that we can return to that level of intimacy.

However, how "to return" has generated more religious ideologies than I care to discuss. I believe that no matter what path we choose in our pursuit of intimacy, our level of intimate communion with our Creator is only obtainable in the Spirit Realm. Despite our eternal quest, Man's free will has hindered his ability to reconnect to his God. Man's choices and decisions sometimes lead to costly outcomes. Some of the difficult experiences we encounter, I believe can be attributed to: our broken spiritual connection with our Creator; complications during our spiritual gestation period; or spiritual labor with a premature delivery. With these thoughts in mind, let us begin to explore the connection between the spiritual birthing process and tragic moments.

Our broken spiritual connection with our Creator has contributed to the many of life's tragic moments. However, I do not believe that life's tragic moments are designed as punishment from an angry God. Much of the religious rhetoric spewed out across the pulpits in churches today uses the wrath

of God to manipulate and control parishioners.

Spiritual abuse is rampant among "spiritual leaders"

using everything from fake prophecies to the Old Testament

stories like the Sons of Korah[7] to maintain power over others.

I have heard Preachers use spiritual intimidation to bully

members into obedience. Some have used spiritual threats of

death to inject fear, into the hearts of those with strong minds,

who would dare question their authority. This message of an

angry God was entrenched in my mind for far too many years.

Growing up in the Holiness/Pentecostal Church every negative

experience was rationalized as punishment from God for some

sin we must have committed.

Jeremiah 29:11 states, "For I know the thoughts that I

think toward you, said the Lord, thoughts of peace, and not of

evil, to give you an expected end."

---

[7] Book of Numbers :16: The story of the Sons of Korah deals with many of
the Children of Israel dying because they challenged Moses' authority

Birthed Out

Setting aside the notion of an angry God, let us explore another hypothesis concerning the reason why we experience tragic moments. This is not a scholarly researched dissertation or a theological debate. This is a supposition, an assumption, a proposition, or a premise if you will. Let us agree that it is not God's desire to see any of His children suffer.

So, with that basic understanding why do we experience so many tragic moments in life? I believe because of our broken spiritual connection with our Creator, we lack spiritual wisdom, which results in our making bad choices and wrong decisions. For the purpose of this discussion, spiritual wisdom is our ability to tune in, listen, and heed Divine guidance from within our own spirit [our spirit, which was already intimately acquainted with our Creator]. God breathed the Breath of Life into Humanity, which gave us direct access to Him through the Vital Force [the Holy Spirit]. Although Humanity fell into sin, we still possess what God breathed into us. Man lost spiritual wisdom [the ability to tap into] the Vital Force, but Man did not lose the Vital Force. The Holy Spirit enables us to reconnect properly with our Creator through Divine guidance.

To simplify this premise, allow me to use an example. When an electrical cord is unplugged, it has no power but it does not stop being an electrical cord. It simply needs an electrical outlet in order to receive and properly use the power available to it. When the prong on an electrical cord becomes damaged an adapter is needed. Although it can fit into the plug without an adapter, its power is limited, its connection can be easily lost, and it is dangerous because the cord is no longer properly equipped to handle the power. In that instance, adding an adapter to the electrical cord is the only way to ensure a safe proper connection.

Due to our broken spiritual connection with our Creator, some of our choices and decisions set in motion a series of events, which lead to tragic consequences. These tragic moments occur not because God is angry and desires to harm us, but because our faulty connection prevented us from tapping into spiritual wisdom concerning the matter. Spiritual

Birthed Out

wisdom comes from a secure and proper connection with our Power Source [God, our Creator].

Our connection can be re-established when we allow The Spirit to restore our perfect union through the Breath of Life [the Vital Force], which came directly from God. The Spirit restores the bond thereby enabling us to tune in, listen, and take heed to Divine Guidance within. We have become so disengaged from the Vital Force [the Breath of Life given to us directly from God] within us until we idolize anyone that we think has any type of ability to "hear or see" into the Spirit Realm.

Whether they call themselves Prophets/Prophetess [using the Holy Spirit], or Psychics [using what they call their Sixth Sense], they are becoming multi-millionaires because we want "A Word" from the Spirit Realm without any effort on our part. I am as guilty of this as you are. We are trying to avoid the spiritual birthing process and we will pay someone else to go through the spiritual birth canal in our stead and just tell us what The Spirit is saying.

Tragic Treasures

We are just like the Children of Israel when they told Moses that they wanted to hear from God for themselves[8]. Moses instructed them on what they would have to endure [the Cleansing Process] in order to put themselves in a spiritual posture where God could speak to them directly. The Children of Israel prepared against the third day. When God showed up in the midst of them and began to speak directly to them, they were experiencing what Adam was accustomed too when he lived in the Garden of Eden. They became so afraid until they stopped God from continuing. Then they begged Moses to talk to God directly and just tell them afterwards what the Lord was saying[9].

From that day forward, the Pastoral Ministry officially began. The Children of Israel did not want to endure what was required [the birthing process] in order to hear from God directly.

---

[8] The Book of Exodus
[9] Exodus 19

Birthed Out

We are still like that today. Being "birthed out" requires spiritual labor and delivery, which results in the birth of God's plan for your life. Inadequate spiritual diets result in developmental delay in the vision or purpose for your life. Whatever we absorb provides spiritual nourishment for our vision, hopes, goals, and dreams.

A spiritual miscarriage leads to the loss of hopes and dreams. In the natural, one of the most dangerous times is during labor and delivery. I believe this is true in the spirit realm as well. Hindrances during labor and delivery could lead to stillbirth. The birthing process will be completed, but if a stillbirth occurs, the vision, purpose, or destiny is already dead before it can come forth. In the spirit realm the vision is dead upon arrival.

Using spiritual wisdom during the birthing process and listening to what The Spirit has to say will help you to avoid tragic consequences that could lead to the spiritual death of your vision, purpose, and destiny. It may seem hard to determine whether the test or trial in your life comes from God or the Adversity, but you must rely upon the Gift of Discernment [an extension of the Holy Spirit] to identify "the Source."

I am not saying that our reconnection with our Creator or being "birthed out" through the Breath of Life [Vital Force] that God breathed into us, with the assistance of the Holy Spirit will prevent all tragedies in our lives from occurring. I am declaring that being in tune, listening, and taking heed to Divine Guidance will lead to avoidance of some heartbreak, deliverance from various dangers, and strength to overcome any adversity that you may have to face.

For those of us who rely upon the Holy Spirit's assistance to operate in good judgment we must pray for the Gift of Discernment [spiritual sensitivity] to clearly distinguish the difference between the presence of Evil and the Potter's Wheel. During our journey towards spiritual illumination we experience life altering events that shift our consciousness to the spirit realm.

Birthed Out

In 1994 I experienced my second spiritual shift. I began having severe pain in my lower abdominal area. For years, I had Pelvic Inflammatory Disease (PID.) It went undetected which resulted in adhesive like lesions on my ovaries, fallopian tubes, and uterus. I had to have a series of surgeries to repair the damage. The first surgery was in 1989 and resulted in the removal of one ovary and fallopian tube. By 1994, the adhesive lesions surrounded my entire reproductive system. They then attached themselves to my small intensives and abdominal wall. My digestive problems escalated and pain increased. The crucial moment came with the news of cancerous cell found on my cervix. With my natural mother's history of uterine cancer a complete hysterectomy was recommended.

I woke up from the surgery with a morphine drip. The pain I felt was excruciating. I was urged to walk off the pain. The hospital discharged me despite my insistence that something was terribly wrong. The pain was unbearable, but I went home.

We didn't know at the time that the surgeon had accidently sliced my small intestines. A general surgeon was called in during the operation to repair it. My digestive system had shut down during the surgery. The doctors assumed it would start working again naturally.

Once at home, all attempts to eat or drink anything ended with vomiting. I spent my days propped on the couch and my nights rolling around on the floor in the living room. I couldn't sleep. I cried, moaned, and groaned throughout the night. Debilitated to the point where my son's father had to bathe me.

After numerous phone calls I was scheduled to be readmitted to the hospital the next day. That night I lay on the floors in tears. I wouldn't make it until Sunrise. I couldn't take the pain another moment. I screamed out to God. Help me. I'm dying. I begged God to heal me. I made a promise that night to pursue His purpose for my life, if he'd spare me. That night I slept. My digestive system started working again after seven days. I never went back to the hospital.

Birthed Out
Divine Spirit,

This road that I am traveling to spiritual illumination has been a long, complex journey. Sometimes I must admit that I have no idea where I fall on the pendulum to spiritual enlargement. Restore my broken spiritual connection. Prepare me for spiritual labor and delivery. At times all I feel is pain and I am unable to distinguish spiritual labor and delivery from a miscarriage. At other times, I feel as if all my hopes and dreams are already gone and my spiritual womb is barren. I must also admit that there have been times in my life when I wished that I could just abort the entire dream myself.

It is difficult to carry ones hopes and dreams to term when you lack the spiritual wisdom required to make the right decisions. I've had too many complications in the Spirit Realm. Equip me with the Spirit of Discernment enabling me to address every difficulty that arises with Divine precision and spiritual sensitivity. Empower me with the capacity to identify the "SOURCE" behind all conflicts, struggles, tests, trials, attacks, or storms. When I do not know the "Source" I cannot effectively wage spiritual warfare. Whenever there is a "Spirit" other than the Spirit of God operating in my life, give me the insight to discern what type of Spirit it is.

&

Where are you on the road to spiritual illumination? Which life altering events shifted your consciousness towards the spirit realm? List those events here and the impact they had.

_____

_____

_____

_____

_____

_____

_____

_____

Chapter Eight

Spiritual Rendezvous

ଔ

I began to experience true healing for my wounded soul through divine encounters with God. I found my way of spiritual communion through what "church folks" called praise and worship. When I returned to church, at first, all I could do was cry. When a song which described everything I wanted to say to God, but didn't know how, touched my heart I cried. I worshipped God from the depths of my soul. His presence engulfed me.

Many times, I found myself in church, on the floor, overwhelmed by His love and forgiveness. I wasn't ashamed to lie there, cry, and ruin my make-up or my hair. I even lost a few hairpieces. Each time I laid myself prostrate on that floor, the Spirit would operate on my battered soul. I would get up looking a "hot ghetto mess", but free from the psychological chains which had bound me.

I craved a manifestation of the Spirit and consecrated an area to the pursuit of His presence at home. I still enjoy sincere praise and worship services, but my spiritual rendezvous' required no audience, other than the Almighty. There have been seasons in my life when I would awake naturally at four a.m. I'd spend the next four hours uninterrupted in my prayer room. Some days, I'd listen to inspirational music and read encouraging words. Other days I'd lay on my mat face down in silence. I listened and wrote in my prayer journal only those words prompted in my spirit.

Years later, I would return to those prayer journals and read in season notes that encouraged me in my current struggle. Sometimes those divine encounters included my earnest cries and screams until I received a spiritual release. In those sacred moments I found myself spiritually naked and unashamed. It was there in His presence where my broken heart mended, my mind renewed, my soul restored, and my spirit lifted.

71

Spiritual Rendezvous

John 4:23-24 says, *"...they that worship Him must worship Him in Spirit and in Truth."*

When I worshipped God from the depths of my soul, in spirit and in the truth of my situation, the truth made me free. The truth allowed me to see, and it helped me to acknowledge, that my entire life up until that point had been a masquerade. I worshipped until truth was revealed unto me.

There are many reasons why we fail to worship in spirit and in truth. Many times, we simply cannot handle the truth of our situation and/or not prepared to have it or Him revealed unto us. Real worship reveals TRUTH. You cannot worship in spirit and in truth and come out of it still believing a lie. All lies are exposed in His presence. Real worship forces you to remove all forms of pretence. When you have worshipped Him "for real," you come out of His presence, fully aware, that a layer of pretense has been stripped from you. After true worship, you can't go back and don the same mask. You are compelled to unveil until you are psychologically

72

uncovered in order to experience the fullness of His presence and complete restoration.

If you allow yourself to become entangled in a yoke of bondage again, you will find it increasingly more difficult to enter into His presence. Many times, we have to labor in prayer for thirty minutes, one hour, or more before we feel what many call a "breakthrough in the spirit." Because we have allowed ourselves to become ensnared again to some situation and/or emotion that hinders us from entering beyond the Veil. The Veil is the spiritual barrier between us and the Divine. We labor in the spirit to get past the "spiritual roadblocks" which often include our fake personas and elevated levels of pseudo strength.

For me, worship enabled me to get past my spiritual roadblocks. Worship is personal and it is private. A congregation is simply not needed in order to worship. Therefore, if you are waiting until you get to church to worship, then you have missed the revelation. There are a few spiritually thirsty souls, which crave worship and will risk embarrassment in front of other church folk for an encounter in

His presence. However, more often than not, true worship is

hindered by the presence of others [spectators and haters.]

The type of fellowship in His presence that sets us free

is rarely found in our churches these days. Do not

misunderstand what I'm saying. The worship experience

encountered in some churches does create an atmosphere

where the Spirit is welcome. Despite that, as a Praise and

Worship Leader [for almost a decade], I must admit, that most

of us do not stay in His presence long enough to be truly set

free from anything. Most of us, are too time conscious and

people oriented to worship God until He heals us. Healing

would require us to remove our mask and many of us just

cannot do that in the presence of others.

Tragic Treasures
Divine Spirit,

I desire nothing more than an intimate encounter with you. I need a manifestation of your presence in my life. In many ways I am like the Children of Israel. I seek your face but many times I'm unwilling to endure the spiritual preparation required to go beyond the veil and commune with you. I have become spiritually co-dependent upon the Church and other so-called Spiritual Leaders for a Word from you. Help to remove the spiritual roadblocks that obstruct my path.

&

Create an atmosphere that will lead to an intimate encounter with the Divine. Record what you've done to prepare yourself for spiritual manifestation in your life.

_____

_____

_____

_____

_____

Chapter Nine
Spoils of War
❧

*"And when Judah came toward the watch tower in the wilderness, they looked unto the multitude, and, behold, they were **dead bodies** fallen to the earth, and none escaped. And when Jehoshaphat and his people came to take away the **spoils** of them, **they found among them in abundance both riches with the dead bodies, and precious jewels,** which they stripped off for themselves, **more than they could carry away: and they were three days in gathering the spoil, it was so much.**" II Chronicles 20: 24-25*

Let's revisit the abundance in riches and precious jewels King Jehoshaphat found lying among the dead bodies. In II Chronicles 20:1-37 you will find King Jehoshaphat confronted with the threat of defeat by a multitude that had come against Judah. He knew from the beginning the Battle could never be won in the flesh, so he went into the Spirit Realm to prepare for the fight of his life. He went on the defensive by fasting and praying before the Battle started.

Spiritual warfare is one of our most powerful weapons. Many of our Battles are lost or won based upon our spiritual posture. Whether we fight on the offensive or defensive plays a great role in how the Battle manifest in the natural. King Jehoshaphat went in the defensive mode before he confronted his enemies. At the threat of War he put on the full armor of God. His prayers ushered him into the very presence of the God where he was able to receive a message.

The message sent to him was that he would not have to fight against this great multitude because the Battle was the Lord's. God would fight the Battle for him. The only requirement was for him to show up for the fight prepared.

King Jehoshaphat employed expert precision when it came to a combative strategy. Judah's preparation centered on praise and worship. Worship was their secret weapon. Worshippers led the way to the Battlefield with praise and their worship drew the presence of God to the scene. God went before them. With God on the scene, the battle was already over before they reached their enemies. By the time, they reached the battlefield God had struck their enemies with a mighty blow causing them to turn on each other.

Spoils of War

Allow me some imaginative liberties. I can see them arriving with tambourines, trumpets, and drums singing praises to the Most High King. Every time they opened their mouths to shout unto the God, He would deliver a mighty blow upside their enemies head.

So what does Jehoshaphat's story tell us?

Our spiritual posture is depended solely upon our receptiveness to Divine guidance. Divine guidance enables us to properly identify the "Source" of the conflict. We should always prepare for War through prayer and fasting, while sending praise and worship before us. When Judah became Worshipping Warriors their victory was secured.

They obeyed the voice of God, showed up covered with a garment of praise, and rewarded with tragic treasures. The Battlefield was full of dead bodies, but scattered among the dead things was "abundance of riches and precious jewels." The abundance was so great until it was more than they could carry away. It took them three days to gather all of the Spoils of War. Imagine they spent three days on the battlefield among death, blood, and guts; but even in the midst of death and tragedy they found an abundance of treasures.

Unfortunately, I was not spiritually prepared for one of the greatest battles of my life. My only child was being seduced by the Streets. In the beginning, I fought my son based upon the traditions of my Holiness/Pentecostal mother and Church Folk. I fought him because it was all about my authority and my control. None of that worked.

I was fighting the wrong person. It was all about my pride and ego. For months, we fought each other and the Enemy just had free rein in both of our lives.

In the beginning, the Adversary began to attack my mind by showing me images of my son dead. Each night as my teenage son ran the streets with his new Crew [five deep] I would stay awake and cry. Terror gripped my spirit to the point I couldn't sleep without keeping my lights on. I locked my bedroom door each night in a feeble attempt to secure enough peace in order to drift off to sleep. Each night I was terrorized by demonic thoughts, voices, and images. It was truly "Terror by night."

In the midst of this demonic attack on my mind and my son's life, I began spending my sleepless, tear-filled, nights locked behind my bedroom door praying and reading scriptures. I would read the same scripture repeatedly, "God has not given us the spirit of fear but of power, love, and a sound mind." I began to read Psalms 91 in its entirety aloud every night:

"He that dwells in the secret place of the Most High shall abide in the Shadow of the Almighty."

Each night as I read the scripture aloud the terror would briefly subside, but the battle raged on. My tears and prayers turned into travailing before God. I would sob uncontrollably during those dark and lonely nights. I realized that despite the prayers of others, no one could fight for my child's life like me. I needed help.

The Spirit of God began to change my focus. Slowly, I turned my attention to the proper Source. I gave up the offensive position and took the defensive stance of protecting my son. I stopped fighting my child and started fighting our mortal Enemy. I was encouraged by members of my church to kick my disobedient son out of the house.

The Holy Spirit spoke against that clearly one day.

I heard the Spirit say, "As long as he stays under this roof he is covered. He is covered by your spiritual posture of prayer. If you kick him out into the streets then you will be giving him over to the Enemy."

Instead of kicking him out, on the days when he chose to leave the house for days at a time I would anoint everything in his bedroom. I would anoint his pillow and pray God would touch his mind. I would anoint his shoes and pray that God would direct his path. I would anoint everything from his clothes, hats, and bed, to his doorpost and window seal while praying in the spirit.

The Spirit directed me to read scriptures from the Book of Ezekiel about having a "new heart." I would speak those scriptures aloud over his life on a daily basis.

Spoils of War

A new heart also will I give you, and a new spirit will I put within you: and I will take away the stony heart out of your flesh, and I will give you a heart of flesh. And I will put my spirit within you, and cause you to walk in my statutes...Ezek 36: 26-27

Those late nights began to strengthen my spiritual core. The night terrors didn't stop until I made them stop. I realized calmness would settle into my spirit when I spoke God's Words aloud.

I began to search the Bible for Scriptures pertaining to my situation. I began to use the Word to command Demonic Spirits in my house to leave. I remember vividly the day the Spirit instructed me to open every door and window. That day Holy Ghost boldness surged through my spirit. I walked through the house in the Power of God commanding Demons to flee. I walked back and forth for hours, from room to room, thrusting those powerful words into the atmosphere. The struggle became so intense until I began to scream the Word aloud at the top of my lungs while anointing every window seal, every entryway, and every doorway on all three sides [like Moses instructed the Children of Israel to do so the Death Angel would pass over when he saw the Blood]. I am sure all my neighbors thought I was crazy, but I didn't care. There was a Spiritual War going on in Apartment D.

I continued to anoint all of my son's possessions. He was furious with me. He would come home to find anointing [olive] oil all over his stuff. That Spring I learned how to wage spiritual warfare when the Spirit of Evil tried to kill my seed. I would repeat this spiritual cleansing ritual for years to come whenever I sensed the wrong type of Spirit in my presence.

To this day, I never move into a new place without my anointed oil and Holy Ghost authority to command every unclean spirit to flee. Spiritual warfare does require more than praying, fasting, and reading the Bible. The Spirit began to give me a strategic battle plan to take back what was stolen from me. At that moment, I felt like David when he returned from one Battle to find his wife and children taken captive by a different enemy[10]. I was greatly distressed, but I inquired of the Spirit and heard him say, "Pursue, and surely you shall recover all."

I determined in my heart if it cost me my life "The Streets" wouldn't have my son. By the Power of the Holy Ghost I decided if he didn't have the strength or desire to fight for himself I would fight for him, not against him. I was finally beginning to sleep at night although my baby was out running the streets. The Spirit would wake me out of a dead sleep and tell me where he was. I would call or just show up. He would be embarrassed and furious. It wasn't about embarrassing him. It was about saving his life. I became a stalker.

I got that stalker instinct from my adopted mother. Old school mothers would walk down the street in their bathrobes, with rollers in their hair, and bedroom slippers yelling their

---

[10] I Samuel 30:3-4, 6, and 8: "So David and his men came to the city, and behold, it was burned with fire; **and their wives, and their sons, and their daughters, were taken captives. Then David and the people that were with him lifted up their voice and wept, until they had no more power to weep.** And David was greatly distressed...because the soul of the people was grieved. **And David enquired of the Lord, saying, shall I pursue after this troop? Shall I overtake them? And he answered him, Pursue: for thou shalt surely overtake them, and without <u>fail recover all</u>.**

child's name, if their child was not home when the streetlights came on. Somewhere along the way, we've lost the ability to fight for our children.

My mother said she would kill somebody over me and I believed her. I became a Stalker in the legal definition of the word with Divine assistance from the Holy Spirit. I became fearless and relentless in my stalking technique. I would show up whether it was at his friend's house or the local teen club hangout. It was Divine intervention. I would pick up his phone book, flip through the pages, and ask the Spirit to reveal his location. I would dial that number and they would always try to tell me that he was not there. By the Power of the Holy Spirit invested in me, I would swear to them that if he didn't come to the phone I would beat the Police to their front door. I possessed the spiritual audacity to defy the Enemy. There is something about a real mother's love for her child, which will cause the most timid woman to change into a ferocious predator, when her baby is in danger.

Spoils of War

It took my son a long time to believe the truth, which was, that the Spirit was giving me all the details needed to stalk him relentlessly. On numerous occasions, the Spirit would wake me from a deep sleep and I would go to the top of the stairs or sit on the couch in the living room only to have him enter the door moments later. One time he left the house claiming he was going to the movies. Moments later the phone rang and a number appeared on the caller ID showing a local Cab company. It only rang once. I didn't pick up the phone. I just looked at the caller ID to see who had called. This was supernatural because my son left the house with his cell phone. He didn't call the Cab from our home phone. I knew instantly that God had revealed his real intentions. I knew at that moment, that he was on his way to a local teen Club that was infamous for Raves and had total access to the drug Ecstasy.

When I called his cell phone he tried to convince me that he was going to the movies. I will never forget what I told him.

I said to him, "I'm on my way to that Club and you had better be on the curb outside when I get there. If you go into that Club, I will come into that club, and I will lay hands on every person in there that stands in my way."

I had my anointing oil with me just in case I had to go into that Club and fight all of those rebellious spirits. He may have been mad, but he was not crazy. When I arrived, he was standing on the curb across the street from the Club furious. At that point, I guess he realized that I was either crazy enough to come up into that Club, or God really was assisting me supernaturally. It got to the point, when I called his friends house, they just gave the phone to him.

During that season he hated me, but God empowered me with a fierce spiritual tracking device that enabled me to stalk him until he couldn't take it anymore. He decided he wanted to move to Kentucky to live with his father. When he called me a stalker, I proudly proclaimed in my spirit I would follow him into the dark streets of Baltimore. He could hate me forever as long as it meant that the Enemy would not destroy him. I still wept bitterly over the rejection I experienced but I kept stalking him. I kept fighting for him. I kept showing up at the battlefield to dreg among the death things to insure that his body would not be found among the corpses. His friends laughed at him and probably taunted him about my behavior, but in the end, those that remained in his life respected the love of his mother. He said he never wanted to see me again. His actions broke my heart into a million pieces, but I thought, if he lives, it will all be worth it.

For almost three months while he was in Kentucky, each time I would call, he refused to talk to me and I would cry. The Enemy would show me our relationship as rubbish among the dead things. Despite what appeared to be "rubbish" I refused to leave the battlefield without my most valuable treasure [my son]. My son returned home after a few months. The Spirit sent me into another mode. The spirit of stalking was gone.

He looked defeated and it was time to build up his spirit. God reminded me that with loving kindness he drew me. Love and kindness would be my next weapon. Love and kindness uncovered the Spoils of War in our both of our lives. His outer transformation was not immediate, but over the next few months his "new heart" grew stronger. Slowly over time, we began to communicate on a deeper level. Then he had a life altering experience that shifted his spiritual consciousness.

After that event we both would begin to discover an abundance of riches and precious jewels among dead things. Within a few days of the event, he made a decision that would change the course of his life for the better. Our focus changed to mending our broken relationship and restoring the trust. I allowed him to candidly discuss any subject with me without judgment, criticism, or rejection. We searched among the rubbish of the two and a half year battle to gleam the rubies, diamonds, and pearls that lay nearby. We are still retrieving the Spoils of War from that battle. We began communicating on a new level with increased openness and candor. Our closeness increased and our love and respect for each other grew to unimaginable levels.

Spoils of War

He expressed his regret and apologized for all of the hurt he had caused me. I apologized for the times when I should have been fighting the Enemy and inadvertently fought him instead. He grew emotionally, mentally, and spiritually into an intelligent, responsible, hard working young man with a promising career.

He loves me with an intensity and sincerity that every mother desires. He has been a constant support to me in every endeavor since that time. I am his number one life coach and cheerleader. I am devoted to him. I would move heaven and stomp through Hell [bare foot in gasoline britches] to protect him. He would drop everything and everyone to come see about me. Out of all the Spoils of War that we gathered from that battle, unconditional love and forgiveness were the greatest treasures discovered.

Tragic Treasures
Divine Spirit,

It's hard to see any treasures in the midst of this tragic mess called my life. I'm overcome by loss, pain, disappointment and constantly reminded of my flaws and failures. Help me to recognize the Spoils of War. Empower me with the strength to pursue tragic treasures in the midst of the dead things of my past. I need your Divine guidance concerning what to pursue. Teach me how to develop a spiritual posture that is receptive to the Spirit's voice. Many of my relationships appear to be rubbish. I will go back again to recover true treasure with the power of the Spirit within me.

&

Make a list of the tragic moments from your past and then list those Spoils of War that you left behind.

_____

_____

_____

_____

Chapter Ten

Treasure Hunt
ᘓ

"But the fruit of the Spirit is love, joy, peace, longsuffering, gentleness, goodness, faith, meekness, temperance against such there is no law." Galatians 5:22-23 KJV

Some of the most precious jewels discovered during my treasure hunt were priceless lessons that taught me how to cultivate the fruit of the Spirit in my life. Once those lessons are embraced our spirit transcends the tragedy and grows in grace. It took a number of years before I realized the effect that each lesson had on my emotional and spiritual growth. As I searched for tangible treasures, priceless rubies, diamonds, and pearls of the Spirit transformed my spiritual core.

It is crucial to embrace the fruit of the Spirit or risk succumbing to the ravishing effects that lingering pain has on the spirit. Persistent agony torments the mind. Enduring

92

headaches harden some hearts and weaken others. Ongoing pain eventually manifests as anger, which then produces bitterness and infects the soul.

Bitterness is a hard root to kill. It is like a cancer which has spread to the bones and robs its victim of life's very essence. The misery associated with unshakable pain displays its distress on the heart through a spirit of depression.

After suffering the effects of depression for many years, I had to pursue and recover indescribable treasures because in my mind all else was fleeting. The accumulation of material possessions did nothing to heal the inexpressible emptiness in my soul. After years of acquiring things I changed the scope of my treasure hunt. Although I bought the house, drove the Lexus SUV, attended Johns Hopkins University for graduate studies, lived in Hawaii, and travelled to Paris, France, none of that strengthened my spiritual core. Once my focus shifted to refining the fruit of the Spirit the healing process was accelerated.

Treasure Hunt

In the pursuit of spiritual treasures I found an abundance of precious gems like: love, joy, peace, and longsuffering. I recovered agape which is unconditional love. It's an undefeatable, unconquerable generosity and kindness that gives freely without asking anything in return. Agape is love by choice, not by force. Agape is love based upon will rather than emotion. I learned to love myself and genuinely love others without requirements. A genuine love surfaced beneath a torrid fear of loss. Instead of allowing fear to prevent my endearment and attachment to others, I sought to love fearlessly in celebration of those who remain.

Love those who remain instead of mourning those lost. You honor those you loved and have lost by living the best life possible. Often tragedy creates such heartache until we become reluctant to love others. We fear that our love will once again be met with pain, suffering, and rejection. But to go through life afraid to love is the greatest tragedy of all. No spirit can prosper without love. Without love forgiveness is impossible. Without love relationships crumble. Without love respect is eroded. Without love hearts harden. Without love minds weaken. Without loves souls suffer.

In the Bible[11], the Apostle Paul mentions that none of the other gifts that we possess mean anything if we don't have love. The foundation of all healing starts with our ability to love. Allow this fruit of the Spirit to rein supreme in your life. With love as a spiritual foundation every proper emotion will be securely established and negative emotions will be scarcely found.

I found a Spirit given expression that flourishes best in hard times: Joy. It isn't a human based happiness that comes and goes. It is divine in origin. It's the subtle inner security that all is well in your soul despite the storm that rages all around you. It's an inner serenity which goes hand in hand with the tranquil state of rest I encountered called peace.

Peace which the Spirit provides leaves tranquility in the soul. Our spirit is unaffected by the outward circumstances

[11] -*Galatians 5:22-23 KJV*

or the pressures of life. It is inner stability in the midst of chaos. It is what I felt the night I came home from work late with my son and our apartment lights had been turned off by the electric company. I did not have the money to pay it. I called a sister-friend of mine and asked if my son could spend the night. I took him over to her apartment for the night. I had no money and no idea what would happen, but I knew that I would be okay. I returned to my dark apartment, lit candles, and read my Bible by candle light. I felt an incredible sense of peace and unspeakable inner joy. The next day I received an unexpected check, cashed it, and paid my electric bill.

If you endure enough tragic moments, your spirit learns longsuffering. Longsuffering bestows the divine strength needed to endure with hope. Longsuffering is not the ability to tolerate foolishness. It is the resilience birthed in our spirit to continue long after others have given up. It's the tenacity to persevere in the face of all adversity. Longsuffering includes tolerance and patience which are gifts given to us by the Spirit to ensure our survival.

Tragic Treasures

All of the emotions that we experience are pure and meant to be felt and expressed. It is only when we express those emotions in such a way that it creates a negative outcome cause for concern arises. There are tragic events that generate justifiable anger which if not eliminated should at least be properly channeled into a righteous cause. Anger should produce positive change. Instead anger uncontained and uncontrolled breeds misapplied hatred which corrupts the spirit with un-forgiveness. Un-forgiveness blocks the fruit of the Spirit from flourishing and leaves its victim spiritually bound.

I purposed in my heart to allow the Spirit to appropriately channel every negative emotion into a righteous outcome. In the past, I've directed my negative emotions towards individuals when those emotions should have propelled me to creative action with positive outcomes. My anger transformed becomes passionate support for others suffering from the results of the same tragic consequences. My fear became vigilant care for those I love. My sorrow became sympathetic concern for the loss suffered by others.

Treasure Hunt

Life can present moments which require persistent pursuit of good in the midst of evil. This expedition is never ending but yields priceless treasures.

Divine Spirit,

Today empower me with a spirit of persistence. It's so easy to give up when surrounded by seemingly overwhelming odds. Sometimes I feel like the Apostle Paul who felt that evil was always present. Teach me how to cultivate the fruit of the Spirit in my life. I have so many mixed emotions that at times feel uncontrollable. I realize that emotions are to be felt but expressed in a way that promotes a positive outcome. Today I take control of my emotions. I will relentlessly hunt for unsnatchable treasures in the midst of every tragedy with the Spirit's s divine guidance.

&

List the Fruit of the Spirit that you will cultivate in your life.

_____

_____

_____

_____

_____

Chapter Eleven

Ultimate Treasure
ଔ

For where your treasure is, there will your heart be also. Matt 6:21

Strengthen your spiritual core: mind, heart, and spirit, in order to obtain the ultimate treasure. That strength is your foundation for overcoming all obstacles.

Many of us understand the importance of feeding our body properly. We spend many hours shopping for just the right clothes that assist us in looking our best. However, we fail to place just as much emphasis on our spiritual health.

Our mind runs rapid with negative thoughts. Negative thoughts embraced often enough penetrate our hearts. "The good man brings good things out of the good stored up in his heart, and the evil man brings evil things out of the evil stored

Ultimate Treasure

up in his heart. For out of the overflow of his heart his mouth speaks."[12]

This means that those thoughts that we embrace whether positive or negative become stored up in our heart [which is the central point of our feelings and intuitions] and in time those thoughts pour from our mouths. Once spoken our words flow in the power given to us by our Creator.

In return if we speak a thing long enough it will eventually manifest in our lives. We must be very careful of those things that we think because "As a man thinks in his heart, so is he.[13]" That's why speaking positive affirmations aloud are so important. Speaking affirmations aloud train your mind to think positive.

At times our minds are cluttered with day to day issues and we need to devote time to train our thoughts. Some of us pray, others meditate. Praying to a Higher Power does allow

---

[12] Luke 6:44-46 [Amplified]
[13] Proverbs 23:7.

100

us to tap into the Spirit realm, but if we never take the time to be quiet and listen for the answers our prayers are pointless.

Meditation is often a way to clear the mind of all thoughts so your soul can tap into what the Spirit is saying. Often the Spirit illuminates the words we should be speaking into our lives. Deep thinkers and those vulnerable to erratic thoughts may want to use some type of mantra to keep their mind focused until they have trained themselves to release all concerns and listen to the Spirit within.

For a number of years I couldn't muster up a positive thought on my own. I began to read or listen to spiritual resources which would have a positive impact on my spirit. Reading positive words contributed to my ability to retrain my mind with positive thoughts. Throughout one season of spiritual strengthen I spoke positive affirmations aloud. During another I wrote the words on sticky 3 by 5 cards and posted them on my bedroom wall. Each morning I would arise and read those cards.

For a number of years I kept what I called prayer journals. I wrote every word spoken into my spirit during times of meditation into those journals. Many times initially those words had no significance to me, but more than once, years later while in the midst of difficult situations I would return to those journals and read words recorded years earlier that spoke to my current situation. It amazed me how the Spirit had provided me the answer to a question that wouldn't be asked for eight years.

Whether it was attending church, reading inspirational books, or listening to sermons on compact disk; I constantly feed positive messages into my spirit to strengthen my spiritual core. I understood the connection between my mind and heart, but to understand the implications that a negative thought has on the spirit goes even deeper.

Our spirit is the vital principle force within us which is capable of connecting to God. However, the strength of our connection can be diminished by the issues that flow from our hearts as a result of negative thoughts.

Tragic Treasures

"Guard your heart above all else, for it determines the course of your life.[14]"

Strengthening my spiritual core required years of prayer, mediation, positive affirmations, fasting, and church attendance. Fasting, prayer, and meditation united created a powerful method of spiritual refinement. Fasting required a sacrificial element of elimination. Sometimes it wasn't food that I had to purge, it was negative influences including: people, places, and things. Church attendance allowed me to fellowship with other Believers and provided one source of spiritual enhancement, but I learned that church attendance, committees, events, titles, and positions are no guarantee or real indication of a strong spiritual core. Strengthening your spiritual core requires private internal effort that busy work can't substitute for.

Divine Spirit,

My spiritual connection with you has been diminished by the issues of life spoken from my very lips. My spiritual core has been weakened due to my neglect. I understand the importance

---

[14] Proverbs 4:23- New Living 2007

of retraining my thoughts, guarding my heart, and strengthening my spirit. It's hard for me to sit still and just listen. Often I've exhausted myself to the point that during any brief moment of inactivity I end up asleep. Today I create a place for spiritual strengthening. I realize that this requires deep internal effort that church attendance in itself doesn't fulfill. Busy work can't substitute for re-establishing a sacred bond with You.

&

What things will you do to strengthen your spiritual core?

_____

_____

_____

_____

_____

Chapter Twelve

Our Soul's Journey
CƷ

Discovering the Spoils of War in the midst of tragedy is a part of our soul's journey. The mind, heart, and spirit make up our spiritual core, but the sum of our spiritual core is our soul. During life's voyage we overlook many of life's lessons meant to enhance our existence, fortify our purpose, and prepare us for our destiny. Overwhelmed by the experience, because they are disguised as obstacles, shrouded in pain, and presented as tragedies, we often ignore tragic treasures. With a rejuvenated spirit and Divine guidance we can embrace those lessons, pursue our treasures, and recover the Spoils of War despite the undesirable package of arrival.

Tragic treasures prepare us for the next level of our soul's journey. These treasures are to be guarded, the Spoils of War cherished, and the lessons learned, incorporated, and shared. When we rise above the tragic consequences of life we

Our Soul's Journey

achieve enlightenment and can effortlessly reach our destiny.

Though our destinies differ with Divine illumination we

position ourselves on the proper course towards fulfilling our

life's purpose with passion.

Once spiritually prepared we can prevent many of life's

stumbling blocks from reoccurring throughout our lives by

grasping the lessons attached the first time. Failure to

acknowledge life lessons often concealed as tragic treasures

hinder our soul's journey. Embrace the hidden treasures and

discover the Spoils of War. Your destiny awaits you in the

midst of every obstacle no matter how tragic.

Tragic Treasures
Divine Spirit,

I realize now that all of life's tragic treasures prepare us for our Soul's Journey. I'm ready to discover hidden treasures in the midst of every tragedy. From this day forward I strive to PURSUE hidden treasures and RECOVER the Spoils of War.

&

List those life lessons you've learned during your Soul's Journey and how those lessons can be applied to help you walk out your purpose and reach your destiny.

_____

_____

_____

_____

_____

_____

CITED WORKS

1. The Holy Bible: The King James Version [KJV]
2. II Chronicles 20:1-37 KJV
3. I Samuel 30:3-4, 6, and 8
4. I Samuel 30:3-4, 6, New King James

About the Author
✄

Dianne Rosena Jones considers herself a *Transformational Life Coach.* She has known that she would write books since she was a teenager. With the debut of *"Tragic Treasures: Discovering Spoils of War in the Midst of Tragedy"*, she embarks upon a new journey using her own life experiences as a gateway to discuss with refreshing candor difficult subjects.

She was born and raised in the Christian Church with more than 30 years involvement in traditional religion. She has held many titles including student, teacher, consultant, trainer, church administrator, minister, worship leader, evangelist, elder, and pastor [very briefly]. Today, she prefers to be known simply as a woman pursuing her God ordained purpose, which is to inspire and empower others to overcome all of life's obstacles by strengthening their spiritual core: mind, spirit, heart, and soul.

She holds a B.S. in Psychology from Morgan State University. She attended Graduate School at Johns Hopkins University.

She resides in Duluth, GA.

For speaking engagements, seminars, or workshops send an email to: rosena@royaltreasurespublishing.com

QUICK ORDER FORM

Postal Orders: Send retail price: $15.99 plus $2.79 shipping
*Add .64 [4% sales tax] for products shipped to Georgia
addresses

**To: Royal Treasures Publishing, P.O. Box 3136, Duluth,
GA 30096**

Payment: Check or Money Order only

Name: _____

Address: _____

City: _____

State:_____ Zip: _____

Phone # _____

Email address: _____

**For Credit Card orders click on the Bookstore link at:
www.royaltreasurespublishing.com**

Or

**Email Credit Card information to:
purchase@royaltreasurespublishing.com**

With email include: Complete name and mailing address, name
on the Credit Card, Credit Card number & exp date, number of
copies, and purchase total.

For additional info email: info@royaltreasurespublishing.com